3rd Edition

Advanced

MARKET
LEADER

Business English Test File

Lewis Lansford

**FINANCIAL
TIMES**

Contents

The recordings for the listening sections of these tests are on a separate *Test Master* CD-ROM, which is free with the *Market Leader Third Edition Advanced Teacher's Resource Book*. They are also on the *Market Leader* website at *www.market-leader.net*.

Entry test

🔊 **1 Listen to a presentation about Oasis Organic Juice International's planned expansion. Choose the best word or phrase to complete these sentences.**

0   The speaker plans to discuss the performance of ....
   a) possible takeover targets   **b)** competitors   **c)** suppliers

1   Zumotina's profits .... last year.
   a) remained steady   **b)** grew   **c)** dropped slightly

2   In the previous three years, Zumotina's turnover increased by ....
   a) more than 50 per cent   **b)** about 15 per cent   **c)** 41 per cent

3   Zumotina has recently had a ....
   a) management reshuffle   **b)** rebranding   **c)** product launch

4   Good Juice's products are ....
   a) sold only in the UK   **b)** relatively expensive   **c)** only partly organic

5   Good Juice's sales are .... domestic.
   a) exclusively   **b)** mostly   **c)** about 50 per cent

6   Last year, Good Juice's profits were .... $1 million.
   a) less than   **b)** about   **c)** a little over

7   Kimura might help Oasis Organic develop a new ....
   a) manufacturing process   **b)** brand image   **c)** market segment

8   Kimura's sales last year were ....
   a) $0.9 million   **b)** about $5 million   **c)** nearly $9 million

9   Most of Hightree's sales are ....
   a) domestic   **b)** export   **c)** direct

10 In the past three years, Hightree's profits have ....
   a) remained flat   **b)** skyrocketed   **c)** slightly increased

A Choose the best words to complete these sentences.

0   Mike is a good salesperson because he's very (persuasive / reserved).

11 Symons Logistics and P2P Parcel have set up a (joint venture / management) to run a new business logistics service in Eastern Europe.

12 The cash flow problems started when some of our (debtors / creditors) were late in paying us.

13 We can't completely eliminate waste but we can (negligibly / significantly) reduce it.

14 The clear, memorable logo has helped the (brand / workforce) become a global success.

15 The drivers' strike (disrupted / soured) distribution for about ten days.

16 Three top managers were laid off but they were given a generous (severance payment / remuneration) as part of the layoff package.

17 Liam is one of the most (irresponsible / considerate) managers I know and his team are all very loyal to him as a result.

18 We always give a (payment / refund) to dissatisfied customers who return a product.

B **Complete the sentences with the words in the box.**

| ~~action~~ | bid | bottom | buck | mile | press | stake | straw |

0 The family took legal .....*action*..... because the toy hurt their child.

19 Kyle Anderson holds a 51 per cent .... in KA Exploration PTY.

20 Don't pass the .... , Leonard. You need to take responsibility for this problem.

21 I respect Paulo because he always does more than he's paid to do. He goes the extra .... every time.

22 The .... conference helped to end the speculation about the company's future.

23 Jones Carter Stone Magnussen has launched a takeover .... for rivals Leech and Beesen.

24 Did you ever get to the .... of that software problem you were having?

25 Having my holiday cancelled is the last .... I can't work here anymore!

LANGUAGE **A** **In the article below, there is one mistake in each sentence. Underline the mistake and write the correct word or words on the lines on the right (26–32).**

Opel aims for growth outside Europe

Opel would like <u>enter</u> a number of markets outside Europe next year in an attempt to boost the car-maker's flagging sales and accelerate its path to profitability.[0]

0 ...*to enter*....

Opel wants to expand into 'at least' six markets in the coming year, probable including China, Australia and Argentina.[26]

26 ....

The ailing car-maker, which narrow escaped insolvency last year, sells only a tiny number of cars outside Europe.[27]

27 ....

A spokesperson said it would take nine to twelve months for Opel to enter that markets, as it would take time to set up dealerships and service networks.[28]

28 ....

The spokesperson also said the company was interest in Chile, Israel and Australia.[29]

29 ....

Opel's European markets are improving everywhere except in Germany, which the company is still reeling from the damage that last year's failed state aid application and sales process caused to the brand.[30]

30 ....

GM tried to sell Opel after the US car-maker went bankrupt but shelved the long-running and very public sales process after business picked out.[31]

31 ....

Mr Reilly said Opel had managed to lift its European market share from 6 to 7 per cent in September, adding that he was expecting a further improve in sales in the next three months.[32]

32 ....

B **Complete the sentences with the correct form of the verb in brackets.**

0   I forgot to bring ....*to bring*.... (bring) a pen. Can I borrow one?

33   I .... (not meet) Dan before we were introduced at last year's sales conference.

34   I .... (talk) on the phone with Ian when the lights went out.

35   Rick .... (work) in Venezuela for ten years when he was transferred to Argentina.

36   Did you remember .... (switch off) the lights when you left the office?

37   If we .... (have) more time, we could have prepared a better presentation.

38   Liam .... (speak) to technical support for two hours but his computer still isn't working.

39   We .... (tell) Jim about his promotion yesterday. He was really happy.

40   Taro learned a lot about manufacturing by .... (spend) time on the factory floor.

READING   **Read the article on page 7 and choose the best answer – a, b, or c – to the questions below.**

41   How much of Priestmangoode's business was conducted with overseas clients last year?
a)   Some of it
b)   Most of it
c)   All of it

42   What is Preistmangoode's line of work?
a)   Design
b)   Transport
c)   Import–export

43   What do the decision-makers in most small British companies think about export?
a)   It's difficult and it rarely helps businesses grow.
b)   It's a great way to grow a business but it can be difficult.
c)   It isn't that difficult but it's also usually a waste of resources.

44   How do 80 per cent of small companies that export set up their export business?
a)   They approach it through careful research and planning.
b)   They start exporting themselves rather than involving another company.
c)   They respond to a request made by a foreign company.

45   What does the article say about most small British businesses?
a)   They don't do a lot of business internationally.
b)   They have too many internal problems to develop export markets.
c)   They're juggling staff all over the world.

46   What does Robin Godfrey help companies do?
a)   Locate partner companies in possible export markets
b)   Develop products specifically for target markets
c)   Identify target markets

47   Which countries are generally less difficult for UK companies to export to?
a)   Ireland and the Netherlands
b)   The US and Ireland
c)   China and the Netherlands

48   What does Godfrey recommend as an important part of research?
a)   Commissioning extensive marketing research in target export markets
b)   Personally travelling to the target export market
c)   Hiring staff from the target export market

49 What allowed Priestmangoode to grow?
a) It dominated the domestic market.
b) It reached out to the global market.
c) It had financial expertise in working in global economies.

50 According to Paul Priestman, what do you have to deal with to export successfully?
a) Language and culture
b) Import–export laws
c) Exchange rates

Some home truths about doing business abroad

By Jonathan Moules

Last year, Priestmangoode, the London-based design consultancy behind Virgin's Pendolino trains and BT's Home Hub broadband box, had no British clients. Its entire £3m turnover came from abroad.

This was a challenge for a business that employs only 24 people – albeit one involved in significant international projects, such as sculpting China's new high-speed rail fleet or laying out the interior of Lufthansa's A380 planes. 'Our staff can be working on projects in six continents,' founder Paul Priestman admits. 'It is a bit of a juggle.' If only more small British businesses had such problems.

The Federation of Small Businesses estimates that as little as 5 per cent of its membership of more than 213,000 companies gains any revenue from abroad, in spite of the general belief that exports are often the best way to grow.

The language barrier, local regulations and fear of not getting paid are all common excuses for not venturing abroad, the business group admits. Those that do take the plunge often end up getting their fingers burnt because they have not properly thought through the process.

Research by the British Chambers of Commerce (BCC) found that only a fifth of those companies that export took a strategic approach. Those that did, however, recorded the highest export growth.

The most common mistake made by companies exporting is that they don't do it for themselves, according to Robin Godfrey, head of the BCC's export marketing research service.

He has encountered this problem many times in his role providing support to would-be exporters on behalf of UK Trade & Investment, the government agency. 'Instead of looking at the world and saying "where should we invest next?", a company will get an e-mail from someone in New Zealand and then rationalise why they should set up an operation over there,' Godfrey explains.

'In fact, the person has contacted them from New Zealand because they are interested in their own business, not the company in the UK, so if that company then goes to New Zealand, they will be doing it for someone else.'

Godfrey's team tries to help UK companies pick their own ideal export country, using a process the BCC calls 'market selection'.

This involves a business owner placing 20 target countries on a board split into four quadrants, dividing them between the big and small markets, then again between those that are easy or difficult to enter.

The idea is to get companies to concentrate first on the easy target markets, most often Ireland and the Netherlands for UK-based companies. Often, only experienced exporters should consider the difficult markets, such as the US and China, Godfrey says.

'It is about being very clear in your head about how you identify your export markets,' Godfrey says, adding that research and actually visiting the country should all be done before taking the plunge and exporting.

Priestmangoode was an exporter from the day it started trading in 1986, because Priestman had already done work for Japanese companies while studying at London's Royal College of Art. He notes that the UK alone would never have provided enough business for the company to reach its current size.

To succeed in exporting you need to be prepared to travel at short notice, Priestman says. 'We have some very, very wealthy clients, who will see what we have done and ask us to a meeting tomorrow in San Francisco or New York,' he explains.

Priestman also believes in the importance of research to understand the nuances of different cultures. Consulate offices can help provide cultural training, for a small fee, he notes. However, he also makes sure he travels with an interpreter.

'The worst thing you can do is to think you know better,' he says. 'In China, for instance, I have learnt a lot from their manufacturers doing things in different ways.'

WRITING You are the Human Resources Manager of a medium-sized firm. The company has been growing and you were hoping to hire a full-time assistant. You advertised the job of Assistant Human Resources Manager and selected Alicia Mendez as the ideal person for the job – someone with excellent qualifications and experience. You made a job offer to Alicia (conditional on approval from the Board of Directors) but the Board has not given their approval due to budget cutbacks. Write an apologetic letter (100–150 words) to Alicia to let her know. Tell her that the situation may change in the next few months but you can't make any promises. Wish her success with her job search and career.

SPEAKING You are going to have a speaking test that will last 10 to 15 minutes. The examiner will ask you to spend five minutes preparing a short (five-minute) presentation. Choose one of the topics below. You may make notes if you wish. After your presentation, the examiner will ask you to elaborate some of your ideas.

> **Topics**
> - A project you have worked on
> - The value of working abroad
> - What companies could do to encourage more women to reach top jobs

Progress test 1 (Units 1–3)

🔊 **2 Listen to an interview with Helen Parker, a training and development consultant. Choose the best answer – a, b or c – to the questions below.**

1 How well does Helen say organisations understand their own training needs?
   a) Usually not very well
   b) Generally pretty well
   c) Often extremely well

2 How does Helen find out what sort of training will be useful to a company?
   a) She asks the management.
   b) She interviews the employees.
   c) She spends time in the company.

3 What is the benefit of the activities she conducts?
   a) They help her see how people work together.
   b) They allow her to understand a company's products or services.
   c) They encourage the management and employees to relax together.

4 How do case studies help Helen?
   a) They allow her to identify the most intelligent people in the organisation.
   b) They let her watch how people react to certain ideas and situations.
   c) They give her an opportunity to encourage people to share their emotions.

5 What do the bridge- or tower-building exercises show Helen?
   a) How groups do or don't cooperate
   b) What learning styles people prefer
   c) Which people are likely to leave the company sooner rather than later

6 Which of these is a feature of the bridge- and tower-building exercises?
   a) The teams must select appropriate materials.
   b) There is a deadline for the project.
   c) The construction must be done without tape or glue.

7 What does Helen say about the building games?
   a) They put people in roles they don't usually perform at work.
   b) They generally reflect how relationships work on the job.
   c) They help improve communication.

8 After the first phase of work in a company, what does Helen do next?
   a) She sets up training programmes.
   b) She makes suggestions for team reorganisation.
   c) She puts workers and managers into 'training teams'.

9 What do coaching and mentoring have in common?
   a) Both build on skills that are already present.
   b) Both introduce and develop new skills.
   c) Both require the financial backing of the company.

10 How is mentoring different from coaching?
   a) Mentoring doesn't require as much commitment.
   b) Mentoring usually requires expert involvement from outside the company.
   c) Mentoring generally has a longer timeline.

VOCABULARY   **A**   **Complete the sentences with the noun form of the words from the box. You will not need all of the words.**

| advise   allow   develop   educate   employ   intern   qualify   recognise |

11   In my final year of university, I had an .... at a Volkswagen plant in Mexico. It was an great experience.

12   I need to ask for some .... about how to make the best possible impression at my interview next week.

13   All employees are given an .... for food and travel expenses when they work away from the office.

14   Nico earned an accounting .... by receiving on-the-job training provided by his company.

15   Adam Reeves has received a lot of .... inside the company for making real improvements through effective training.

B   **Complete the conversation with the words and phrases in the box.**

| emissions   energy   eyes   in agreement   off   panels   slouching
staring   technology   wave |

Seth   I heard you gave a presentation on renewable ....[16] this morning. How did it go?

Piet   Not very well. Martin asked me to do it just yesterday and I wasn't really prepared.

Seth   Oh, that's a shame. What happened?

Piet   Well, I started off talking about the need to reduce carbon ....[17] and at first I thought people were nodding ....[18] but actually they were nodding ....[19]!

Seth   Did you have a chance to talk about fuel-cell ....[20]? That's your area of expertise.

Piet   Only at the very end. It seemed like everyone was more interested in ....[21] power and solar ....[22] and I'm not really an expert on those.

Seth   No, that's more Martin's area, isn't it?

Piet   When we'd been going for about half an hour, everyone was just ....[23] in their seats. A couple of people asked interesting questions and I thought I was recovering but then the catering people started setting up for coffee break so of course everyone was letting their ....[24] wander over to that.

Seth   Oh, dear.

Piet   Then I noticed that Martin was sitting at the back of the room with his arms folded across his chest, ...[25] at me and acting as though he was offended by my bad presentation!

LANGUAGE **A** **Match the sentence beginnings (26–30) with the best endings (a–e).**

26 Don't worry about organising the training schedule,

a) I merely typed it up.

27 I don't think Beth wrote this;

b) Lawrence already did it.

28 Several people worked on this but

c) it was primarily Ian who put it together.

29 Because it's difficult, not everyone has finished the training course but Lisa

d) Jane probably did it.

30 Stan did most of the planning and

e) successfully completed one last year.

B **Each of these sentences contains an expression that's wrong. Cross out the incorrect word and write the correct one.**

31 If we're going to turn this company around, we need to connect the spots and understand that all of our problems are somehow related. ....

32 We don't want to allow workers to home their skills at our company and then take their expertise somewhere else for more money. ....

33 Your theory makes a lot of sense but it's completely divorced from practising. We simply don't work that way! ....

34 It's important to rejog teams from time to time even when there isn't a problem. It keeps ideas fresh. ....

35 When he said my input was 'academic', I think he was using the word in the pejorating sense. ....

C **Choose the correct words to complete these sentences.**

36 Most people understand the need to move away from (the / —) fossil fuels but actually doing it will be very difficult.

37 (An / The) airline industry around the world has suffered in the recession.

38 We need to identify (a / the) sympathetic person in middle management who would be willing to take on a mentoring role for at least the next two years.

39 (The / —) US is often seen as a tough market by UK companies.

40 Building (a / the) personal network is extremely important for graduates.

SKILLS **A** **Put the sentences into a logical order to make a conversation.**

a) **Sam** I thought your face looked familiar! I was there, too. I'd love to talk to you sometime soon about something I'm working on.

b) **Mia** Not at all. I'm Mia Leeman. I'm with Kumatori Brake Company in Osaka. Sam, you might like to meet my colleague Nori Okazaki. He works on brake systems for Toyota.

c) **Mia** Excuse me. I'll let you two keep on talking but I'm afraid I have to make a quick call.

d) **Sam** Yes, that would be good. So you're based in Osaka, is that correct?

e) **Sam** Hello. I'm Sam Soames. I'm in marketing with Toyota UK. Do you mind me asking where you're from?

f) **Nori** Nice to meet you, Sam. I met some of your colleagues at the Paris Motor Show.

g) **Nori** OK, Mia. See you later. Sam, we should do lunch one day this week.

h) **Nori** Not quite. Mia is in Osaka but I'm based at one of our factories, in Thailand.

41 .... 43 .... 45 .... 47 ....

42 .... 44 .... 48 .... 48 ....

B **Complete the conversation with the words and phrases in the box.**

> agree   clarify   could consider   keep going on
> keep our options open   meant   would be

A Liam's leaving next week and we still don't have a replacement.

B We ....[49] sharing out his work between ourselves.

A Sorry but could you ....[50] how that would work?

B Well, I just ....[51] that you and I could divide Liam's work. You take half, I'll take half.

A I'm not sure I ....[52] with you there. Wouldn't it be way too much for us?

B I know I ....[53] about this but since he lost his two biggest accounts, he just hasn't been that busy.

A Let's ....[54]; we need to consider hiring a replacement.

B Fair enough. Another option ....[55] to just wait and see what happens.

READING **Read the article and decide if these statements are true or false.**

56 Siemsa Cataluña was founded as a wind turbine manufacturer.

57 Spain's wind-generation capacity increased by about 40–50 times between 1991 and the writing of the article.

58 Few companies produce more wind energy than Iberdrola.

59 Photovoltaic energy hasn't been badly affected by recent changes in market conditions.

60 Between 2005 and the writing of the article, Spain's PV capacity increased by 3,456 MW.

61 A number of factors has meant that since October 2008, new investment in PV technology has virtually stopped.

62 In the year before the article was written, GES's revenues decreased to 25 per cent of their previous level.

63 Ingeteam was acquired by GES but the acquisition led to layoffs.

64 Several solar energy companies have delayed going public until the economic situation improves.

65 The Spanish government deregulated electricity prices in early 2010 to stimulate investment.

Renewable energy: Cloudy forecast for solar power

By Mark Mulligan

Founded in 1982 as Siemsa Cataluña, the company now known as Global Energy Services started life as an engineering services provider to petrochemical complexes in the country's industrial zones.

In 1991, Siemsa Cataluña was bought by Gamesa, then a fledgling wind turbine manufacturer and wind park developer, under whose ownership it diversified into most generation technologies.

'When we became part of Gamesa, there were about 400 or 500 megawatts of wind-powered generation capacity in Spain,' says Ricardo Moro, GES Chief Executive. Today, there are close to 20,000MW scattered around the country, putting Spain's among the world's highest per capita producers and users of wind energy.

In the process, Gamesa, which fed much of that development, has become a global leader and Iberdrola, the electricity generator, is the world's number one in terms of wind power capacity.

However, investment in the segment has dropped sharply in the past two years as falling demand and lower wholesale power prices have combined with scarce financing and regulatory uncertainty, forcing companies to rethink their plans.

Solar energy using photovoltaic (PV) cells has been the hardest hit, caught between tight credit conditions, government austerity and an official crackdown on market abuses and overinvestment. From 44MW of installed capacity at the end of 2005, Spain today has about 3,500MW of PV capacity, according to the European Commission. However, most of that was installed before October 2008, when feed-in tariffs for new plants were slashed. These cuts, plus the financing crisis, capacity quotas and uncertainty about pricing regimes have put the brakes on fresh investment in the sector.

In spite of its broad geographical and business diversification, GES felt the impact: Mr Moro attributes a 25 per cent drop in revenues last year, to €530m ($730m), mainly to the absence of new photovoltaic installation contracts.

The company was also forced to lay off hundreds of workers. In Spain's industrialised Basque region, specialist engineering groups also suffered. Bilbao-based Ingeteam, among the world's biggest manufacturers of electrical and mechanical components for wind farms and solar parks, noted a marked drop in sales. Stock market volatility and the eurozone debt crisis also added to the uncertainty, forcing a clutch of solar energy groups to postpone planned initial public offerings in Madrid.

Although bringing some order to the photovoltaic segment and reaching temporary accords on pricing and capacity with thermo-solar and wind park operators, the government remains under pressure to bring clarity to longer-term energy policy. Its reluctance to deregulate electricity prices completely continues to create unease among potential investors. Analysts say it has little choice but to let market forces decide.

WRITING

You are responsible for organising a stand at an important trade show. On 15 July you ordered from a stationery company 1,000 promotional giveaway bags with printed matter about your products as well as pens with your company name and other items. On 17 November, three weeks later than scheduled and only three days before the trade show, 100 bags arrived. You phoned the company and explained that the order was 900 bags short. They promised to deliver the additional bags in time for the trade show but they failed to do so. Write a formal e-mail of complaint (150–200 words). It should start and finish with the appropriate salutations.

Structure your e-mail as follows:

* Write to your contact at the company, Ms Lisa Lawrence.

* Explain briefly why you are dissatisfied with the service.

* Set out the details of what happened.

* Describe the consequences: you lost the opportunity to make contact and communicate with important customers, which could affect your business.

* Point out that the paperwork for the order and the packing list that came with the delivery specified 1,000 rather than 100 bags and so the error should have been picked up at the supplier's end.

* Say that you've now decided to cancel the purchase. Ask the supplier for a full refund of your payment.

Progress test 2 (Units 4–6)

🔊 3 **Bill Wilson works for an advertising agency. He has asked his colleague, Alison Bates, for some advice. Bill is worried about the behaviour of their manager, Steve Parks. Listen to their conversation and decide whether these statements are true or false.**

1 Bill is worried because he's too busy.

2 Bill is making a formal complaint to Alison.

3 Bill is concerned that Steve has lied.

4 Steve and Bill often go on business trips together.

5 Steve and Bill visited a shopping mall together, on business.

6 Steve bought an expensive bag for a client.

7 Steve paid for a present for his wife with his company credit card.

8 Steve has a budget to buy meals and presents for clients.

9 Steve encouraged Bill to pay for personal items with his company credit card.

10 Bill is worried that Steve's behaviour could hurt the company.

11 Bill wants Alison to talk to Steve about the problem.

12 As well as misusing his credit card, Steve is basically an incompetent manager in Bill's view.

13 Alison thinks Bill should talk to Steve's manager immediately.

14 Alison suggests that Bill speaks to Steve about his concerns.

15 Bill seems unlikely to take Alison's advice.

VOCABULARY **A** **Complete the articles with the words in the box.**

> bid   commitments   drop in   individual   influence
> juggle   market   set up   viral   word of mouth

Web marketing in China

A recent .... [16] study in China has found that.................... [17] marketing – for example video clips that circulate on social networking sites – is taking off more there than in Western markets. The .... [18] of blogs and other user-generated consumer reporting is rapidly increasing and consumers trust .... [19] views and opinions which speak to their .... [20] requirements more than advertising.

The home office

Knight Corporate Finance is a boutique business advisory firm that was .... [21] by Paul Billingham and Adam Zoldan. However, the closest thing they have to an office where you could.................... [22] for a visit is Home House, a members' club in central London. And they only use it as a place to host meetings. Both men .... [23] a busy professional life and the demands of a young family. Working from home is a .... [24] – so far successful – to keep their .... [25] both at home and the office.

B **Match the sentence beginnings (26–30) with the best endings (a–e).**

26 The CEO was forced to resign after he became mired in

27 A junior researcher stumbled across

28 At the trial, the CEO said that he wanted to come clean about

29 The researcher said that it had taken her several weeks to work up

30 After a new CEO had taken

a) evidence of serious accounting irregularities and reported it to the authorities.

b) the guts to report what she'd found.

c) the bad decisions he'd made and simply clear the air.

d) the helm, the company was able to put the past behind it and rebuild its image.

e) allegations of serious accounting fraud.

LANGUAGE

A **Decide whether the underlined clauses are defining (D) or non-defining (N).**

31 Bob Hatterson is someone who I can really trust to do a great job.

32 Peter James, a manager at Marks & Spencer, has some fresh ideas about marketing.

33 This distribution issue isn't a problem we're going to be able to solve easily.

34 Ikea, the giant of the flat-pack furniture industry, has been a global success for decades.

35 The website, launched only two months ago, has already generated hundreds of thousands of euros in profit for the company.

36 We want to avoid marketing products aimed only at teens.

B **Choose the best words to complete the sentences.**

37 By (working / to work) for a variety of employers, I've gained a lot of experience.

38 I'm not laid back enough (living / to live) as a freelancer. I'd always worry about the next job.

39 He's a (hard-working / hard-work) manager so he gets a lot done.

40 It's hard to keep up to speed but I enjoy (doing / to do) it.

41 People who employ you expect you (being / to be) on call all the time.

42 I tried to stop John making the payment but he (couldn't / wouldn't) listen to me.

43 Hiding the truth was a mistake. I (shouldn't / wouldn't) have done that but I did.

44 If I had been in your position, I (should / would) have asked for help.

45 Larry said he (couldn't / shouldn't) force Liam to stop taking big risks.

READING

Read the article on page 17 and choose the best answer – a, b or c – to the questions below.

46 What do companies not understand well, according to recent research?
   a) What attracts workers to join a company
   b) What makes workers want to stay in a job
   c) What makes employees want to perform well in a job

47 Which of these things does the research show?
   a) Workers and employees have different ideas about what encourages loyalty.
   b) Employers aren't interested in retaining talent.
   c) Employees don't consider it important to be motivated.

48 Which of these was among employees' main motivations?
   a) Recognition of individual achievement
   b) The company's ethics
   c) The remuneration package

49 What do employees think of the way their abilities are applied to their work?
   a) Companies don't take full advantage of employees' abilities.
   b) Companies expect too much of employees.
   c) Companies are basically good at making use of employees' talents.

50 How have workers responded to the economic downturn?
   a) A large percentage of people have accepted jobs way below their ability level.
   b) Many have developed new expertise that they can apply to their work.
   c) They have had to conceal lack of ability in order to compete in the job market.

51 What would cause 25 per cent of workers who aren't actively looking for work to change jobs?
   a) Disappointment with their current position
   b) The opportunity to join a company with a strong brand
   c) A job that offered more pay, a good career path or more flexible working conditions

52 Why does Brian Wilkinson say companies need to motivate workers to stay?
   a) Because workers have skills that are valuable to the company
   b) Because a well-motivated workforce is more productive
   c) Because the danger of head-hunting by the competition is high

53 What does Brian Wilkinson recommend companies invest in?
   a) Cost-cutting technology
   b) Retaining key staff
   c) Making employment more flexible

54 How does Brian Wilkinson recommend companies deal with the ageing population?
   a) Attract young talent with extensive training packages
   b) Freeze the retirement age
   c) Plan to use short-term personnel solutions

55 What does the article say about employees working away from the office?
   a) It's increasingly popular with workers.
   b) Many employers are already strongly encouraging it.
   c) It isn't likely to be a permanent solution for most companies.

Staff motivation misunderstood

By Brian Groom

Employers are failing to understand properly what motivates their employees to continue working for them, according to recruitment industry research.

A survey of 800 people by Randstad, the recruitment company, revealed a mismatch between what employers think will retain talented staff and what employees say will make them stay.

Employers ranked the main factors driving people to stay at a company as its brand, culture and the benefits package offered. But employees ranked the most important factors as the level of pay followed by training and development, a good career path and flexible working conditions.

Randstad's report, which examines current and future patterns of employment, found half of employees surveyed felt their skills were being under-utilised, even though 23 per cent had improved them during the past 18 months.

It has labelled this group 'Generation R'. During the economic downturn, a third of permanent staff and a fifth of interims and contractors have raised their skills to cover additional responsibilities, often because organisations have not hired new staff. The recession has also resulted in around 10 per cent of people taking up positions that do not fully utilise their skills.

Brian Wilkinson, head of Randstad UK, said: 'Our report highlights that there is a gap between what organisations think will motivate their key talent to stay with them and what their employees actually say will retain them. The research also showed that a quarter of workers who are not actively looking would consider changing employer if something attractive came up.'

It was important that organisations acted now to resolve this gulf in understanding, otherwise they risked losing talented people who had acquired new skills and made themselves more valuable, he said. 'For many organisations it will be a fine balancing act between investing to hold on to key staff and minimising the overall labour cost base by building in more flexible employment strategies.'

Mr Wilkinson added that while organisations were focusing on pressing issues, they must not lose sight of long-term trends that pointed towards skills shortages, particularly as the number of people of working age declined and the population aged. Raising the retirement age would help organisations, he said, but many would also need to adopt human resource strategies that made greater use of temporary and interim skills as well as technology. 'Remote working has been spoken about for many years, but many people will expect to do more work this way in the future, so employers will need to adapt to access the best talent.'

SKILLS **A** **Read the introduction to a presentation. Write the letter (a–h) of the correct technique next to the number (56–60) of the extract from the text. You will not need all the techniques.**

Good morning. <u>My boss is an optimist. He says 'The glass is half full.' His boss is a pessimist. She says 'The glass is half empty.'</u> My name's Becky Mendez. I'm a marketing consultant and I say <u>'Your glass needs re-sizing.'</u>[56]
<u>According to inventor Edwin Land, 'Marketing is what you do when your product is no good.'</u>[57] <u>For all of us who work in marketing, that's a pretty strong statement, isn't it?</u>[58]
But is Land right? Are we working in marketing because our <u>product is no good</u>[59]?

Now, you may or may not know that Land was the inventor of the hugely successful Polaroid camera. You probably didn't know that <u>in the mid 1990s, the company had an annual revenue of $2.31 billion</u>[60]? Obviously Polaroid was doing something right …

a) Involving the audience
b) Referring to surprising facts or figures
c) Emphasising key words
d) Using humour
e) Calling for action
f) Quoting someone
g) Inviting agreement
h) Telling an anecdote

56 .... 59 ....

57 .... 60 ....

58 ....

B **Complete the sentences with the words in the box.**

| go   'm listening   sense   sound   understand |

Greg   Shelly, hi. Good to see you.

Shelly   We need to talk about this afternoon's presentation, Greg.

Greg   I ....[61] you're feeling a bit anxious about it.

Shelly   Yes, more than a bit anxious. I don't think we're ready for it!

Greg   I ....[62]. Please ....[63] on.

Shelly   We're presenting together but we haven't practised!

Greg   I'm not sure I ....[64]. We've given this sort of presentation quite a few times before.

Shelly   Yes, but not in front of 300 people. I'm not sure I want to go through with it.

Greg   You ....[65] as if you're really worried about it.

Shelly   I am!

WRITING   **You are planning a monthly update meeting later in the week with three people you manage: Uma, Phoebe and Neil. The day and time have already been agreed. Write a polite, neutral e-mail (150–200 words) to them. Include the following information.**

- Time: 10:00–12:00. Place: Room 247. Need to start and finish on time. (People have been late in the past and have wasted time during the meeting.)

- Team should update you on all of their projects.

- Everyone should bring their latest sales figures for presentation.

- Larry Collins, your regional manager in Manchester, has resigned at short notice; need to discuss interim duties to take up the slack; come prepared to make suggestions regarding any affected work.

- Need to discuss (not for the first time) the continuing problem of the kitchen area (not everyone is cleaning up after themselves; someone is leaving dirty dishes in the sink daily).

- Offer the opportunity to ask questions and share comments and say you're looking forward to the meeting.

Progress test 3 (Units 7–9)

🔊 4 **Kate from the UK and Pascal from France have just finished business school and want to start their own business. They have no capital so they are looking for investors. Listen to their phone call and choose the best word or phrase to complete these sentences.**

1 Pascal has spoken with .... venture capital firms.

   a) 10   b) 11   c) 12

2 The problem is that Kate and Pascal lack ....

   a) experience   b) education   c) a business plan

3 Pascal's meeting with one venture capitalist was ....

   a) very successful   b) cancelled   c) rescheduled

4 Kate was advised to seek venture capital after the business ....

   a) makes some revenue   b) has an online presence

   c) makes €100,000

5 If the business can get some good .... , it may convince investors to invest.

   a) suppliers   b) advertising   c) customers

6 Kate's parents said they could invest ....

   a) €1,000   b) €10,000   c) €100,000

7 Kate doesn't want to take her parents' money because they are close ....

   a) to bankruptcy   b) to retirement   c) relatives

8 Their business plan says they need ....

   a) €5,000   b) €50,000   c) €500,000

9 Kate suggests they reduce .... by working from home.

   a) risk   b) start-up costs   c) salaries

10 Pascal says he doesn't want to lose ....

   a) any money   b) credibility   c) control of the business

A **Complete each sentence with the correct preposition or particle.**

11 How did the accountant get away .... the scam for ten years?

12 I'm sorry, but these figures just don't add ....

13 The strike has been called .... because a settlement has been reached.

14 I think the success of this project can be put down .... a lot of hard work and a lot of luck.

15 We've run out .... time. We'll have to submit the proposal as it is.

B Delete the words in each sentence that can be omitted in informal conversation.

Carl Are you going to the meeting this afternoon?[16]

Lisa Yes, I am going to the meeting this afternoon.[17]

Carl Did you see Clayton this morning?[18]

Lisa No, I didn't see Clayton this morning.[19]

Carl He won't be at the meeting. Anyway, I'll see you there.[20]

C Match the statements (21–25) with the best responses (a–e).

21 I've been made employee of the month for the first time ever!

22 When will Bertrand have his part of the project ready?

23 Elise is top salesperson again.

24 I think you should tell someone your boss has been lying.

25 I think we should get new laptops for the whole family.

a) What's the use? Everyone's doing it.

b) Well, what do you know?

c) How long is a piece of string?

d) Do I look like I'm made of money?

e) So, what else is new?

VOCABULARY

A Complete the sentences with the words in the box.

catch-up	debrief	deposit	hammer	investment	nit	relief	trade

26 Barton breathed a sigh of .... when he'd finished his presentation.

27 It took several days to .... out the details of the contract.

28 After the negotiations were complete, the team took some time for a .... to talk about what had gone well and what hadn't.

29 Let's schedule a .... call for first thing Monday morning so we can bring each other up to date on the past few days' work.

30 Brett is good to work with. He always has a small .... or two on our presentations but in the end he definitely improves them every time.

31 The property .... side of the business isn't doing as well as we'd like.

32 We've put down a ten per cent .... on our new offices and we'll move next month.

33 We're excited that the fair .... part of our business is doing really well.

B Choose the correct words to complete these extracts from the *Financial Times*.

Canal Plus, the French pay-television operator majority-owned by Vivendi, has renewed its interest in buying a stake in Digital Plus, its Spanish counterpart, as it steps up its international (expansion / widening / bridging)[34] plans.

Herman Van Rompuy, the EU's permanent president, drew up budget rules that would allow fines to be imposed on eurozone members that fail to bring their (economy / national / digital)[35] debt levels down.

Mr Dobson said the (geographic / fast-moving / bank)[36] diversity of the inflows and its broad range of investment products made the business more resilient to broader market turbulence.
'We have been adding more front-office, client-facing staff in the private bank,' he said. 'Because we have a strong financial (economy / trade / position)[37], we have been able to invest consistently while others were cutting costs.'

Ken Downing, fashion director at department store Neiman Marcus, says: 'In a (challenged / short-term / down)[38] economy, designers want to make clothes that create desire, that make women want to shop.'

Head Start allows first-time buyers to purchase a new property with an 80 per cent mortgage and a 5 per cent (loan / deposit / down)[39]. Barratt pays the other 15 per cent and buyers have up to 10 years to pay back the interest-free (funding / savings / loan)[40].

SKILLS

Choose the best word or phrase to complete the conversations.

Conversation 1

A So, who'd like to get the ball ....[41]?

B I'm thinking along the ....[42] of a web pop-up window.

C I was just going to say ....[43]!

A Here's another ....[44] – a social networking viral ad.

B That's a ....[45] idea!

Conversation 2

A Would you mind ....[46] me about the explosion at your factory in Bilbao?

B Are you ....[47] there was an explosion? Because we've never said that.

A Are you ....[48] there was an explosion?

B We've never said there was an explosion.

A I'll ....[49] the question. Was there an explosion at your factory in Bilbao?

B Our press release said there was an incident.

A With all due respect, you haven't ....[50] my question.

Conversation 3

A I was wondering if you could deliver a bit ....[51] than next month.

B We could, ...[52] you paid in cash.

A I'd have to ....[53] my supervisor first. She'd have to ....[54] the payment terms, you see.

B I'll wait to ....[55] from you, then.

41	a)	to move	b)	rolling	c)	going
42	a)	way	b)	idea	c)	lines
43	a)	that	b)	this	c)	those
44	a)	thought	b)	suggest	c)	concept
45	a)	one	b)	computer	c)	cool
46	a)	saying	b)	telling	c)	speaking
47	a)	asking	b)	questioning	c)	saying
48	a)	denying	b)	answering	c)	understanding
49	a)	finish	b)	rephrase	c)	put
50	a)	said	b)	answered	c)	replied
51	a)	quick	b)	closer	c)	sooner
52	a)	to provide	b)	provided	c)	provide
53	a)	check with	b)	check out	c)	check
54	a)	do	b)	agreed	c)	confirm
55	a)	hear	b)	have heard	c)	hearing

Read the article on page 23 and choose the best answer – a, b, or c – to the questions below.

56 Who has found that the government isn't managing consultant costs well?
   a) A non-government independent organisation
   b) A consultant
   c) The National Audit Office

57 What has the National Audit Office never done before now?
   a) Calculated the cost of consultants to non-government bodies
   b) Used non-government consultants
   c) Taken over the management of government consultants

58 What has cost the government £215m?
   a) Permanent managerial staff
   b) Temporary managerial staff
   c) Research on spending

59 Why does the cost of government consultants appear to have gone down?
   a) Control of consultant costs has been improved
   b) There have been improvements in record-keeping
   c) Fewer consultants have been hired

60 What can be concluded from the NAO's report?
   a) It's unlikely that the downward trend in consultant spending will continue.
   b) A sustained downward trend in consultant spending appears to have begun.
   c) The hiring of consultants is likely to increase in coming years.

61 What is the predicted result of new rules for hiring consultants?
   a) Individual consultants will have to cut their fees in half.
   b) The cost of consultants to the government will remain steady.
   c) The government will cut spending on consultants by about 50 per cent.

62 What will be one likely result of the new rules?
   a) Consultants will still be hired but they won't be called consultants.
   b) They will provide a more or less permanent solution to the problem.
   c) More permanent managerial posts will be created.

63 Which best describes the brief of many consultants to the government?
   a) It lacks a clearly defined objective.
   b) The terms of payment are unclear.
   c) It includes ongoing appraisal.

64 What is one reason given for the hiring of consultants?
   a) It costs far less to pay a consultant than to pay a regular employee.
   b) Consultants are generally far more efficient than permanent staff.
   c) There are limitations on the number of permanent staff.

65 What does the NAO say is needed to keep spending down?
   a) More clearly defined briefs
   b) Better management
   c) Shorter contracts

Answer key

Entry test

Listening (10 marks)
See page 36 for audio script.

1 b 2 a 3 c 4 b 5 b 6 a 7 c 8 c 9 a 10 c

Vocabulary (15 marks)

11 joint venture
12 debtors
13 significantly
14 brand
15 disrupted
16 severance payment
17 considerate
18 refund
19 stake
20 buck
21 mile
22 press
23 bid
24 bottom
25 straw

Language (15 marks)

26 probable, probably
27 narrow, narrowly
28 that, those
29 interest, interested
30 which, where
31 out, up
32 improve, improvement
33 hadn't met
34 was talking
35 had been working
36 to switch off
37 'd had / had had
38 has been speaking
39 told
40 spending

Reading (10 marks)

41 c 42 a 43 b 44 c 45 a 46 c 47 a 48 b 49 b 50 a

Writing (15 marks)
See page 42 for Examiner's notes.

Dear Ms Mendez

Re: Post of Assistant Human Resources Manager

As you know, your appointment to the post of Assistant Human Resources Manager was conditional on approval from the Board of Directors. I am very sorry to have to tell you that we have been unable to get this approval. Although having an Assistant Human Resources Manager would be of enormous benefit to our company, we do not have the budget to fill the role at the present time.

I very much regret having to withdraw our job offer since your qualifications and experience would have made you the ideal person for this post.

There is a possibility that the situation may change within the next few months and if this is the case I will let you know. However, please be aware that we cannot offer any guarantees.

I wish you every success in your job search and in your future career.

Yours sincerely

Speaking (15 marks)
See page 42 for Examiner's notes.

Progress test 1

Listening (10 marks)
See page 37 for audio script.

1 a 2 c 3 a 4 b 5 a 6 b 7 b 8 a 9 a 10 c

Vocabulary (15 marks)

11 internship
12 advice
13 allowance
14 qualification
15 recognition
16 energy
17 emissions
18 in agreement
19 off
20 technology
21 wave
22 panels
23 slouching
24 eyes
25 staring

Language (15 marks)

26 b 27 d 28 c 29 e 30 a
31 spots, dots
32 home, hone
33 practising, practice
34 rejog, rejig
35 pejorating, pejorative
36 —
37 The
38 a

39 The

40 a

Skills *(15 marks)*

41 e   42 b   43 f   44 a   45 c   46 g   47 d   48 h

49 could consider

50 clarify

51 meant

52 agree

53 keep going on

54 keep our options open

55 would be

Reading *(10 marks)*

56 False   57 True   58 False   59 False   60 True

61 True   62 False   63 False   64 True   65 False

Writing *(15 marks)*

See page 42 for Examiner's notes.

Subject: Promotional giveaway bags

Dear Ms Lawrence

I'm writing to express our dissatisfaction with your service. Your company failed to deliver our complete order on time.

We received delivery of 100 promotional giveaway bags on 17 November, three weeks later than scheduled. However, the order was for a total of 1,000 bags. I immediately called your customer services department and asked for the missing 900 bags to be delivered in time for our trade show on 19 November. I pointed out that, as it was your mistake, it was your responsibility to correct it. I was promised that the additional bags would be delivered in time for the show. However, we did not receive this delivery until 25 November. The trade show was over by then. As a result, we lost the opportunity to make contact and communicate with important customers, which could have serious consequences for our business.

The paperwork for the order and the packing list that came with the 100 bags both specified 1,000 bags rather than 100. Your company failed to check that the order was complete and failed to respond to our request to correct the mistake. We therefore request that you refund our entire payment.

Yours sincerely

Progress test 2

Listening *(15 marks)*

See page 38 for audio script.

1 False   2 False   3 False   4 True   5 True

6 False   7 True   8 True   9 True   10 True

11 False   12 False   13 False   14 True   15 False

Vocabulary *(15 marks)*

16 market

17 viral

18 influence

19 word of mouth

20 individual

21 set up

22 drop in

23 juggle

24 bid

25 commitments

26 e   27 a   28 c   29 b   30 d

Language *(15 marks)*

31 D   32 N   33 D   34 N   35 N   36 D

37 working

38 to live

39 hard-working

40 doing

41 to be

42 wouldn't

43 shouldn't

44 would

45 couldn't

Reading *(10 marks)*

46 b   47 a   48 c   49 a   50 b   51 c   52 a   53 b

54 c   55 a

Skills *(10 marks)*

56 d   57 f   58 g   59 c   60 b

61 sense

62 'm listening

63 go

64 understand

65 sound

Writing *(15 marks)*

See page 42 for Examiner's notes.

Subject: Meeting on Thursday

Dear Uma, Phoebe and Neil

Our monthly update meeting will be held this Thursday at 10:00 in room 247. I'd like you to come prepared to give an update on all of our projects and also to present your latest sales figures. We've had problems starting and finishing on time in the past so please arrive a few minutes early and plan to stay focused for the entire two hours.

I've recently learned that Larry Collins, our regional manager in Manchester, has unfortunately resigned at short notice. We'll need to discuss interim duties to take up the slack left by Larry's resignation so please come prepared to make suggestions about how to deal with any work that may be affected by Larry's departure.

Finally, we need to discuss again the continuing problem of the mess in the kitchen area. Despite the fact that we've discussed this several times already, someone is still leaving dirty dishes in the sink almost every day. This is unacceptable and whoever's doing it needs to take responsibility.

If you have any questions or comments, please let me know. I'm looking forward to seeing all of you on Thursday.

With best regards

Progress test 3

Listening (10 marks)

See page 39 for audio script.

1 c   2 a   3 b   4 a   5 c   6 a   7 b   8 c   9 b   10 c

Language (15 marks)

11 with
12 up
13 off
14 to
15 of
16 Are you
17 going to the meeting this afternoon
18 Did
19 see Clayton this morning
20 Anyway, I'll
21 b   22 c   23 e   24 a   25 d

Vocabulary (15 marks)

26 relief
27 hammer
28 debrief
29 catch-up
30 nit
31 investment
32 deposit
33 trade
34 expansion
35 national
36 geographic
37 position
38 challenged
39 deposit
40 loan

Skills (15 marks)

41 b   42 c   43 a   44 a   45 c   46 b   47 c   48 a
49 b   50 b   51 c   52 b   53 a   54 c   55 a

Reading (10 marks)

56 c   57 a   58 b   59 b   60 a   61 c   62 a   63 a
64 c   65 b

Writing (15 marks)

See page 42 for Examiner's notes.

Re: Order 901010 – Wiring harnesses

Dear Mr Tyler

I'm writing to confirm what we discussed in our phone call this morning.

As we discussed in our call, you have approved the prototype and you're happy to proceed with the first order. We can supply 30 wiring harnesses assembled to the specifications supplied in job document 355a. We're pleased to offer you a price of $36,000 ($1,200 per harness).

Please remember that if you increase your order to 60 parts or more, we can bring the unit price down to $1,075.

Regarding delivery charges, I'd like to point out that I forgot to mention on the phone the delivery fee of $120. I hope this is acceptable.

As for payment and delivery, our usual terms are a 50 per cent payment on order and the balance, including delivery charges, on delivery, with 30-day credit terms. We can supply the full order not later than 15 November.

As we discussed, we may have problems getting some components from our suppliers. If this happens, we will notify you within five days of the order date and at that time give you the option to cancel the order and receive a full refund of your deposit.

Could you please confirm your order by e-mail as soon as possible.

Do contact me if you need any more information or have any questions.

Looking forward to doing business with you.

Yours sincerely

Progress test 4

Listening (10 marks)

See page 40 for audio script.

1 c   2 a   3 a   4 b   5 a   6 c   7 a   8 b   9 b   10 c

Vocabulary (15 marks)

11 some fine-tuning
12 the slack
13 Over-assigning
14 foul
15 chances
16 amends
17 our engagement
18 a broad shift
19 trawling
20 trying to come up with
21 hawking
22 broadcasting
23 netting
24 gauging
25 proving

Language (15 marks)

26 a ton
27 an arm
28 grass
29 overnight
30 bets
31 What we did next was make our catalogue searchable online.
32 The person you need to write to is Lisa Reed, the regional manager.
33 The reason why we increased production was to fill all of our orders.
34 What the workers have achieved is something completely unexpected.
35 It was the software update that solved the battery problem.
36 d   37 a   38 b   39 e   40 c

Skills *(15 marks)*

41 b 42 d 43 a 44 e 45 c
46 b 47 d 48 c 49 e 50 a

51 on
52 to
53 over
54 for
55 by

Reading *(10 marks)*

56 b 57 c 58 a 59 c 60 a 61 e 62 a 63 d 64 b 65 c

Writing *(15 marks)*

See page 42 for Examiner's notes.

Dear Mr Leeson

Re: Invoices 490440 and 491005

I'm writing to inform you that invoice 490440 for £3,890.23 dated 27 August and invoice 491005 for £2,944.59 dated 27 September are still unpaid. I attach copies of these invoices for your information. As you know, our agreed payment terms are 30 days from the date of the invoice.

In view of our good commercial relationship in the past, we'd like to resolve the matter amicably. We'd ask you to settle your account within ten working days. In the event that you have already paid the invoices, please ignore this reminder.

If there is a problem with the quality of the printing or binding which has caused you to withhold payment, please contact us immediately at the telephone number below and we can resolve the issue.

Should you fail to pay these invoices by the stated date, then we may have no alternative but to review your account with us, which would mean that we would no longer be able to supply your company with printing services.

Best regards

Exit test

Listening *(10 marks)*

See page 41 for audio script.

1 c 2 a 3 b 4 b 5 c 6 a 7 b 8 c 9 a 10 c

Language *(15 marks)*

11 ~~enough confident~~ confident enough
12 ~~Which~~ What
13 ~~all above~~ above all
14 20 years' ~~the~~ experience
15 ~~of~~ which
16 ~~experience~~ experiencing
17 ~~switching~~ to switch
18 must <u>have</u> been
19 would<u>n't</u>
20 ~~of money out~~ out of money
21 you are ~~ready~~
22 ~~It's~~ Is it
23 ~~hoping~~ hopping
24 ~~Who~~ What
25 sure <u>to</u> include

Skills *(15 marks)*

26 f 27 h 28 g 29 e 30 b 31 d 32 a 33 c
34 point
35 thing
36 e-mail
37 discussion
38 question
39 alternative
40 start

Reading *(10 marks)*

41 b 42 a 43 c 44 a 45 b 46 b 47 c 48 a
49 b 50 a

Writing *(15 marks)*

See page 42 for Examiner's notes.

Proposal to carry out research into Internet use in Kenya

Background

Internet access in Kenya has recently increased greatly. There are three main reasons for this. One is the recent connection of an undersea fibre optic cable in Mombasa. The second is the resulting drop in the price of wholesale Internet access in the region, which will mean more net-based business will soon be possible. The third is the growing core market of computer-literate people who understand the benefits of computer and Internet use. The client has requested a detailed analysis of the cities of Mombasa and Nairobi that will help them develop a strategic plan for marketing their low-cost palmtops in Kenya.

Aims

- To provide a clear understanding of the Kenyan palmtop computer market
- To identify the factors influencing future demand
- To forecast the market penetration of Internet-ready palmtops into Kenya over the next five years
- To identify the areas with the greatest strategic importance to the client company
- To compile a database for each area

Methods

Both quantitative and qualitative data will be collected to establish current patterns of Internet/computer use, as well as future trends. We will analyse this data, using several different techniques. This data will enable us to draw up a profile of existing users showing how they use their computers and the Internet. It will also provide the basis for a strategic model that will help the client prepare detailed marketing plans and target potential users.

Speaking *(15 marks)*

See pages 42–43 for Examiner's notes.

Government spends £1.5bn on consultants

By Nicholas Timmins

The British government and its associated non-government independent organisations spent £1.5bn on consultants last year but the government has no effective strategy to manage the spending better, the National Audit Office has warned.

The main government departments spent £790m on consultants, while associated non-government bodies spent another £700m – the first time the NAO has calculated that figure.

In addition, the government spent another £215m on interim managers, individuals hired to do a job that would normally be a permanent post.

Central departments' consultancy costs were down by £125m on four years ago, when the NAO last analysed the figures, but most of the fall was likely to be due to better recording of costs rather than improved controls on use, the NAO said in a report on Thursday. That suggests that some of the reduction is not sustainable.

Francis Maude, the Cabinet Office minister, has announced a string of controls on the appointment of consultants, which he said on Wednesday was likely to halve the bill, saving £800m.

But the NAO said that while the measures were having 'a short-term impact', as a long-term strategy they 'could lead to the displacement of costs elsewhere', with hirings redefined so that they no longer counted as consultancy, the audit office said. The controls 'cannot be an effective ongoing approach to managing spending', it said.

Despite the best efforts of the Office of Government Commerce, which offers skills and guidance on best practice, there had been limited progress on recommendations made four years ago on the more effective use of consultants.

Data on their use, type of consultancy, number of interims employed and length of contracts remained poor. Departments were bad at defining what they wanted, they still paid overwhelmingly on day rates and for time and materials used, not for the outcome of the work, the NAO said. There was very little evaluation of consultants' work during projects, or afterwards, or even whether the results were then used, even where consultants had performed well.

Half of departments identified headcount restrictions as a principal cause of their use of consultants, who do not count as permanent staff. But with a freeze on civil service recruitment in place, it is not clear that pressure will ease.

In addition, departments had done nothing like enough to plug the skills gaps that led them to hire consultants in the first place. Demand for the top two services – programme and project management – had been rising rather than falling, now accounting for 60 per cent of all consultancy.

The Cabinet Office is now collecting monthly data on the use of consultants. Any contract above £20,000 requires ministerial sign-off and any longer than nine months requires Cabinet Office and Treasury approval. But much more effective management was needed to produce a sustainable cost reduction, the NAO said.

The Management Consultancies Association said it backed many of the NAO's recommendations, including rigorous evaluation of achievement and payment by results.

You work for Car Electrics, a company that supplies wiring and electrical components for cars. You had a phone call this morning with Mr Dean Tyler of Tyler Custom Car Conversions (TCCC), a company which converts petrol automobiles to run with electric motors. You negotiated a deal for your company to supply a shipment of wiring harnesses to TCCC. Read your notes from the phone call and write an e-mail (200–250 words) summarising what was agreed in the negotiations. Include a subject heading.

Order number: 901010

— Mr Tyler confirms that they approve the prototype and we can proceed with first order.

— Order: 30 wiring harnesses assembled to TCCC's supplied specifications (job document 355a)

— Payment: $36,000 ($1,200 x30)

— Delivery: $120 (Forgot to mention this on the phone!)

— Terms: 50% on order, balance (including delivery charges) on delivery (30-day credit terms)

— Delivery: to TCCC not later than 15 November

— NB: We may have problems getting some components from our suppliers. If this happens, we will notify TCCC within five days of the order date and give them the option to cancel with full return of deposit.

— NB: An order of 60 parts or more will bring unit price down to $1,075

Progress test 4 (Units 10–12)

🔊 **5 Listen to a presentation on the Critical Path Method (CPM). Choose the best answer – a, b, or c – to the questions below.**

1 What is CPM based on?
   a) Software analysis
   b) Management analysis
   c) Mathematical analysis

2 What information does CPM analyse?
   a) Project activities, their duration and their dependency
   b) Project activities, project personnel and skills available in the team
   c) Project activities, required end date and supply chain factors

3 What does the speaker say about house building?
   a) The framing depends on the foundations.
   b) The plumbing depends on the electrics.
   c) The foundations depend on the plumbing.

4 What does CPM calculate?
   a) The most efficient technology for each activity
   b) The 'path' of the project from start to finish
   c) The projected effect of possible delays

5 What is a 'critical activity'?
   a) One that will change the end date if it goes off schedule
   b) One that depends on other activities
   c) One that the project team can't agree about

6 What is an activity with 'total float'?
   a) One that will delay the entire project if it's late
   b) One that is optional and doesn't have to be done
   c) One that doesn't affect the overall schedule

7 What does the 'critical path' show?
   a) The shortest possible schedule
   b) The longest possible schedule
   c) A reasonable 'average' schedule

8 How does CPM help managers?
   a) It helps them minimise the number of people required for a project.
   b) It helps them run a project as efficiently as possible.
   c) It helps them link schedules and budgets.

9 What does a Gantt chart do?
   a) Clearly shows activity assignments
   b) Clearly displays the critical path
   c) Clearly shows suggested options for dealing with possible delays

10 Where are project elements often displayed in a Gantt chart?
   a) In the bars
   b) Along the top of the chart
   c) On the left-hand side

VOCABULARY **A** Complete the sentences with the words and phrases in the box.

> a broad shift   amends   chances   foul   our engagement   over-assigning
> some fine-tuning   the slack

11 Our system works well enough but it needs .... to make it more efficient.

12 If we take all of .... time out of the schedule, we may run into trouble if there are unexpected delays.

13 .... critical tasks to stronger team members can cause real problems with schedules.

14 Every time something unexpected slows us down, Dean shouts .... and starts rearranging the team.

15 If you're constantly behind schedule, ... are your project plan was over-optimistic.

16 We're hoping to make .... with the team at ATC and start doing business together again soon.

17 We're developing some plans for improving .... with social media.

18 There's been .... in attitudes towards debt in the past few years.

B Complete the text with the words and phrases in the box.

> broadcasting   gauging   hawking   proving   netting   trawling
> trying to come up with

I own an independent bookstore. Last year, I spent months ....[19] the
Internet and ....[20] a good idea for launching an online side to my business.
There are plenty of websites out there ....[21] anything you can imagine and
....................[22] huge discounts but it's hard to imagine most of them ....[23]
more than a few hundred pounds a year and I'm sure some of them are losing money.
It was easy to decide which sites I liked the look of but ....[24] the success
of any online business – even huge companies like Amazon – is impossible. Last month,
I stopped worrying about what everyone else was doing and launched a simple website.
It isn't yet ....[25] to be the making of my online business but I have a lot of
ideas for developing it.

LANGUAGE **A** Choose the correct words to complete the conversation.

Alicia I'm so tired of carrying this laptop. It weighs (a million / a ton / forever)[26]!

Eric And it cost (a head / a foot / an arm)[27] and a leg, too, didn't it? Business travel is never easy!

Alicia Anyway, I heard you launched the YX-248. How's that going?

Eric It hasn't taken off in the mainstream yet but there's a lot of (grass / tree / plant)[28] roots interest in it already. It's all over the blogs.

Alicia Not every product can be an (entrenched / offensive / overnight)[29] success. Did you launch with the black case or the red one in the end?

Eric We're hedging our (tracks / bets / wins)[30] and offering both from the start.

Alicia Oh, that sounds good.

B Rewrite these sentences, starting with the words given.

31 Next, we made our catalogue searchable online.

What we ....

32 Lisa Reed is the regional manager – you need to write to her.

The person ....

33 We increased production to fill all of our orders.

The reason why ....

34 The workers have achieved something completely unexpected.

What the workers ....

35 The battery problem was solved by the software update.

It was ....

C Match each sentence (a–e) with the correct rhetorical device (36–40).

Are parasites a problem for your business?

That's a no-brainer – a question which has an obvious answer.[a] Parasites – the mosquito that bites you, the cowbird that leaves its eggs in other birds' nests – take but they don't give anything back.[b] Watch out for them.[c] A mosquito bite can completely ruin your holiday – or your business.[d] We'll look for them, we'll find them and we'll get rid of them.[e]

36 Exaggerating for dramatic effect ....

37 Giving a definition ....

38 Illustrating a point with examples ....

39 Repeating a grammatical form ....

40 Using imperative forms ....

SKILLS

A Put the sentences into a logical order to make a conversation.

a) **Helen** I'm sorry but we have to deal with cash flow, too, and we expect our customers to pay their bills on time.

b) **Helen** I'm phoning about the outstanding payment on our last invoice. As you know, our credit terms are 30 days and payment is now well overdue.

c) **Helen** I think we can work with that.

d) **Ken** Yes, I'm aware of all that but we can't spend money we haven't got.

e) **Ken** As I mentioned earlier, we've been seriously let down ourselves. I expect to send you a cheque on 15th March. Will that be acceptable?

41 ....

42 ....

43 ....

43 ....

45 ....

B **Complete the conversation with the sentences (a–e) below.**

A   When is your company going to clean up the site?

B   .... ⁴⁶

A   Actually, I'd like you to answer the question now.

B   .... ⁴⁷

A   Who does have it?

B   .... ⁴⁸ You see, we have a dedicated clean-up team and they're still evaluating the situation.

A   Are you saying there isn't a schedule for the clean-up?

B   .... ⁴⁹ The schedule will be their responsibility.

A   OK, can you tell us anything about the nature of the chemicals at the site?

B   .... ⁵⁰

a)   I'm pleased you raised that point.
b)   Do you mind if we deal with that later?
c)   I'm afraid that's not really my field.
d)   I'm afraid I don't have that information to hand.
e)   As I've already said, the clean-up team is evaluating the situation.

C **Complete the sentences with the words in the box.**

by   for   on   over   to

51   Beatta just said something I'd like to comment ....

52   I'd like to add .... what Joanna just said.

53   Let's go .... the action points before we finish.

54   I have a question .... Liam.

55   Can I just check who's doing what and .... when?

READING **A** **Read the article on page 29 and choose the best option – a, b, or c – to complete the sentences below.**

56   McGeough and von Spreckelsen realised their five-year plan .... expected.
  a) as   b) later than   c) earlier than

57   Bapco Closures eventually opened their production facility ....
  a) in Canada   b) in the UK   c) in the US

58   Bapco .... most start-ups.
  a)   fought for survival longer than
  b)   turned a profit at about the same time as
  c)   had a better idea than

59   Robin Klein thinks start-ups should ....
  a)   clearly understand their business model
  b)   generate revenue above all else
  c)   focus on their core business

60   Duncan Grierson financed his start-up by ....
  a)   pretending to remodel part of his house
  b)   remortgaging his house
  c)   drawing a salary from a part-time job

B Match the sentence beginnings (61–65) with the best endings (a–e).

61 Peter McGeough

62 Robin Klein says the founders of Skype

63 Stefan Glaenzer

64 Duncan Grierson

65 Last.fm

a) worked on the core business idea and waited for the business model to become clear.

b) didn't earn money from his company for three years.

c) paid a big return to investors in just two years.

d) backed a successful online music business.

e) did consultancy work to generate income.

Find the finance – and hold your nerve

By Jonathan Moules

Back in 1998, Peter McGeough and Henning von Spreckelsen took their families out to dinner to tell them that they were quitting their steady jobs at carton-maker Tetra Pak because they had a brilliant solution to the leaky milk bottle top.

They had a five-year plan that involved buying a factory in Norwich to make their sophisticated plastic caps and fully expected to sell their venture, Bapco Closures, in eight years.

In fact it took them eight years to get someone to buy their idea and even then revenues were only £168,000 for the year. The plans, both for the UK factory and the target market, bit the dust much earlier, after the milk industry pulled its support for Bapco's product development. When McGeough and his team finally found a market for their product among food producers in North America, the founders had to go back to their eight angel investors for a further £4m of cash to build a factory in the US. 'It was a big ask,' McGeough admits. But what he and his team did have was the entrepreneurial survivor's instinct.

'I could say it was stubbornness or bloody-mindedness,' McGeough says. 'We wanted to prove to the dairy industry that they were wrong but we also believed that we could come up with a solution.'

Most start-ups do not battle on for as long as Bapco. The majority of would-be entrepreneurs fall by the wayside much sooner, exhausted by the stream of rejections or perhaps attracted back to the perceived security of a salaried post. Even a successful technology start-up can expect to be on a diet of baked beans and goodwill for three years, according to Robin Klein, founding partner of seed funding business The Accelerator Group (TAG).

The length of time new entrepreneurs have to spend without salary may increase in the coming years, particularly if, as forecast, the recovery of the economy remains sluggish and the banks remain unwilling to lend. The question then becomes how best to survive, what can be cut and where else a business owner can get cash to keep trading.

The temptation may be to rush into anything that can generate revenues for the business. McGeough admits that in the lean years he and his co-founders at Bapco would do whatever consultancy work they could to keep a roof over their families' heads.

Chasing revenues might not be the best strategy, according to Klein, who notes that some of the most successful start-ups, such as Internet telephony provider Skype, were far more focused on getting their product right.

'Skype had no revenue for years but the founders and backers were very clear that, if they could get millions of users, there was a business model lurking in there somewhere,' Klein says.

A much better use of time is to focus on stripping out the costs of the business, according to Stefan Glaenzer, a serial entrepreneur and investor who founded Ricardo.de, Germany's largest online auction company, before moving to London in 2000 to support other technology start-ups.

Living frugally is easier for young companies run by young people, which typify many of Glaenzer's more high profile investments. For instance, in 2005 he became the first person to back Last.fm, the online music business based in London's East End, which was sold just two years later to US media business CBS for $280m (£176m).

Duncan Grierson, who went without a salary for three years while developing his household waste recycling business Sterecycle, not only worked from home but rented his spare bedroom and his living room floor to bring in cash. He also borrowed £25,000 from the bank under the guise of renovating his kitchen, using the money to pay his mortgage – a move that would certainly be more difficult in the current financial climate. The journey is not over for Sterecycle but Grierson has now built his first waste management plant in Rotherham and is processing up to 100,000 tonnes a year for three local authorities that have signed 10-year contracts.

The good news for those considering taking the plunge is that the cost of starting businesses is less with the reduction in technology costs, through innovations such as Internet telephony and freeware, software that is free to use.

You can make your own luck and survive longer by choosing good backers, according to Glaenzer. 'It all comes down to the selection of the right partners, be it mentors, advisers or seed investors,' he says.

It is helpful if your financial backers have a passion for what you are trying to achieve, Glaenzer notes. 'If you have someone who is only looking at the return on investment, they might not go the extra mile when you need them,' he says.

WRITING   You work in the accounts office of a printing firm. A small book publisher – Leeson House – has failed to pay two invoices. Use your manager's notes below to write a formal e-mail (150–200 words) to Mr Leeson, requesting payment.

Please write to Mr Leeson re: unpaid invoices

Invoice 490440 – £3,890.23 – 27 August

Invoice 491005 – £2,944.59 – 27 September

Terms: 30 days from invoice date

Good commercial relationship in past

Request settlement within 10 days

Problem with printing and binding? Call us.

If he fails to pay, will review account – may stop printing for him.

Exit test (General review)

🔊 6 **Listen to a presentation by Robert Innes, CEO of Talbot Engineering. He's speaking to workers at the opening of a newly-refurbished factory in Leeds, UK. Choose the best answer – a, b, or c – to the questions below.**

1   What does Innes say about the history of the company?
   a) The company is more than two hundred years old.
   b) In the past ten years, the company has changed from being complacent to being competitive.
   c) It used to be family-owned and that helped create the company culture.

2   Who needs to ask if the company is running as smoothly as possible, whether communication with customers is as good as it can be and how services can be improved?
   a) All of Talbot's employees
   b) Talbot's management
   c) Talbot's customers

3   What does Innes say he wants to give Talbot's customers?
   a) The best value for money
   b) A relationship that lasts years rather than months
   c) Clear goals

4   How does Talbot prefer to work with customers?
   a) To fill their orders accurately and quickly
   b) To collaborate on research and development
   c) To carry out market research on behalf of customers

5   What can workers at Daisy Hill expect to see?
   a) Executive managers who want to understand production processes
   b) Quality control inspectors who want to see how work is carried out
   c) Customers who want to see how products are made

6   What does Innes say Talbot factors into its production costs?
   a) The human side of production
   b) Depreciation of equipment
   c) Regular pay increases

7   How much of its production does Talbot export?
   a) 14 per cent
   b) 40 per cent
   c) 44 per cent

8   What can we infer from Innes's mention of China?
   a) Talbot's main competition will be from Chinese companies.
   b) Talbot hopes to manufacture more cheaply in China for import to the UK.
   c) Talbot hopes to increase its sales outside of the UK.

9   What is the current status of Talbot's production in China?
   a) Some joint ventures have already been set up.
   b) Several factories have already commenced production.
   c) A timeline has been established for outsourcing work to Asia.

10 What opportunity will some Daisy Hill workers be offered?
   a) The chance to take on middle management jobs in Chinese factories
   b) The chance to be trained in the latest manufacturing techniques
   c) The chance to go to China to provide training

LANGUAGE

Find and correct the error in each sentence.

11 I don't feel enough confident to stand in front of an audience and answer their questions. ....

12 Which our competition doesn't do is provide good after-sales service. ....

13 The training weekend was, all above, a great chance for people to get to know one another. ....

14 Our company has 20 years' the experience of working in a global marketplace in at least 20 different languages. ....

15 We've sold about 28,000 units to date, which about 26,000 are still in use. ....

16 By experience day-to-day life in one of your target markets, you can really begin to understand your potential customers. ....

17 Last Friday, the office lights were left on at the end of the day, so please remember switching them off before you leave this afternoon. ....

18 Fred must been a good salesperson when he worked for us because there was a sudden drop in sales revenue after he left. ....

19 Even if we'd sold twice as much, it would have made any difference – we'd still be way below the forecasts. ....

20 We've run of money out so I'm afraid we may be looking at having to file for bankruptcy. ....

21 I'm as ready to finish this project as you are ready. ....

22 It's just me or are there a lot of people sitting around trying to look busy? ....

23 David is hoping mad about Lucien leaving without giving any notice and taking a job with the competition. ....

24 Who Lindy brought to the company was a good eye for design and a lot of international experience. ....

25 When you're scheduling the conference, be sure include plenty of time after each session for questions and answers. ....

SKILLS **A**

Match the questions and statements (26–33) with the best responses (a–h).

26 I don't suppose you know any good places to eat near here, do you?

27 I've been based in Singapore for the past three years.

28 Let me make sure I understand you correctly. You're saying the Leeds location won't remain open?

29 Sorry, could I ask you to give me those figures again?

30 The best course of action is to get some focus groups together over the coming weeks.

31 I do think it's important we offer someone the job today.

32 What do you think I should do about accepting the promotion offer?

33 Sorry to interrupt, I just wonder if you're going to tell us what you plan to do about the situation in Mumbai?

a) You have to weigh up the pros and cons.

b) I'm not sure I agree with you there. I think we need to make some of these decisions ourselves.

c) If I could just finish what I was saying, I'll talk about that situation in a minute.

d) Let's not make any hasty decisions. We need to think this through a bit more.

e) Sure. I said $49,300 in the first quarter and $39,030 in the second.

f) As a matter of fact, I went to a fantastic curry house last night.

g) No, what I meant to say was the Leeds operation will be scaled down.

h) I was there not long ago, actually.

B Complete the sentences with the words in the box.

| alternative | discussion | e-mail | point | question | start | thing |

34 OK, from your .... of view, we should scrap this idea. Correct?

35 You know, a funny .... happened to me the other day while I was waiting for a client to arrive at my office for a meeting.

36 Could you please confirm your order by .... as soon as possible?

37 Let's go round the table once and then open the .... up.

38 Sorry, could you just repeat your .... because I don't think everyone heard.

39 We may have no .... but to ignore the problem and continue with the project as planned.

40 We only have 45 minutes so let's make a ....

READING   Read the article.

The careerist: 'The key to ambition is understanding your motivations'

By Rhymer Rigby

Ambition is an oddity in the workplace toolkit. It varies across cultures and organisations, with some people finding it distasteful, while for others it is the single most important factor in shaping their career. Given that it can sometimes make the difference between success and failure, is it possible to take steps to boost it?

Can I turn myself into a serial entrepreneur or CEO of a dozen companies?
Probably not, says Cary Cooper, Professor of Organisational Psychology at Lancaster University. 'Really driven people like entrepreneurs who keep doing it again and again usually have a drive that comes from something traumatic in their childhood.' However, he says, for most people not having this is a good thing. 'No matter how successful [driven people] are, they'll never quite believe it and they'll never be satisfied – their success doesn't make them happy; they just keep going.'

What about cultivating a more healthy ambition? Instead of looking at obsessives who are working themselves into the ground, you are better off taking your cues from people who seem to enjoy what they are doing and appear genuinely enthused by it. These people tend to stick with one thing or in one area and their good fortune is usually a mixture of interest and hard work.

So how do I boost my ambition?
'The key to ambition is understanding your motivations – if you can understand these, that makes sense of everything else,' says Corinne Mills of Personal Career Management. 'I was talking to a banker the other day who said he was motivated by money. But actually when we dug around a bit we discovered he was really motivated by security.'

There are two other very important ways to boost your drive: 'You need to start to take risks,' says Ms Mills. 'Ambitious people do not just sit in the same job. Apply for new positions, network and really get yourself out of your comfort zone.'

Risk-taking is something that virtually all ambitious people do far better than also-rans. Finally, you should not make excuses. Rather than moaning about your lot, you need to look at whatever it is you are doing and do the best you possibly can.

For example, if you wait for the perfect role for your talents, you will wait forever.

Is ambition all about money and power?
John Drysdale, Managing Director of Momentum Executive Development, says he is witnessing a shift in the way people view ambition. 'Of course people still work hard but they're seeing ambition less in terms of just money and power. You want to get to the top but you want people to respect you, too. I think the paradigm is shifting – particularly as we're currently looking at the consequences of too much uncritical ambition.'

Is an extra dose of ambition all I need to revitalise my career?
No. While talent without ambition can be cute, ambition without talent results in the kind of tragi-comic mini-megalomaniacs you see booted out of *The Apprentice* in early rounds. It is probably best to think of it as a catalyst that makes your other attributes perform better – but the raw material needs to be there first.

Now choose the best option – a, b or c – to complete the sentences below.

41 According to the article, ambition is .... success in business.
   a) necessary for
   b) not always important for
   c) ultimately harmful to

42 Most people probably .... needed to experience the sort of success that strongly ambitious people often achieve.
   a) can't learn the traits
   b) don't understand what's
   c) already have the skills

43 Cary Cooper believes that strong ambition often ....
   a) is harmful to children
   b) leads to failure
   c) makes people unhappy

44 People who have 'healthy' ambition generally ....
   a) enjoy their work
   b) try a lot of different things
   c) pretend to be happy

45 Tapping into a healthy ambition is a matter of understanding ....
   a) your past
   b) what you really want
   c) competition

46 Comfort is generally .... of ambition.
   a) a common result
   b) the enemy
   c) a key motivation

47 Less ambitious people tend to take .... than very driven people.
   a) less advice
   b) more time decision-making
   c) fewer risks

48 Finding a job that perfectly matches your skills .... ambition.
   a) isn't a realistic
   b) should be your highest
   c) will unlock your

49 John Drysdale believes that in the past, people tended to view ambition more as a desire for .... than they do now.
   a) hard work
   b) money and power
   c) respect

50 Ambition is useful only if you also have ....
   a) real ability
   b) clear earning potential
   c) a sound business plan

WRITING

You represent a firm of market research consultants which is proposing to carry out research into Internet use in East Africa for the producer of a very low-cost, Internet-ready palmtop computer (the client company). Look at the informal notes and draw up the first part of a proposal in three paragraphs (200–250 words), with subheadings as shown. You do not need to specify details such as costs and deadlines for the work.

Background

Reasons for growing Internet access in East Africa (primarily Kenya):

1) Undersea fibre optic cable recently connected in Mombasa, Kenya

2) Wholesale Internet access prices have dropped radically, meaning more net-based business will become possible

3) Refurbished PCs donated to African schools may have created a growing core market of computer-literate people

Client requests analysis of the cities of Mombasa and Nairobi in order to develop a strategic marketing plan

Aims

Client needs:

- Clear understanding of Kenyan market + factors influencing demand

- Forecast for next five years

- Which area most important? Compile database for each.

Methods

Collect quantitative + qualitative data — establish current patterns, future trends

Use several different analysis techniques to draw up profile of existing users, how they use computers/the Internet

Provide basis for strategic model — help client develop marketing plans, target potential users

SPEAKING

You are going to have a speaking test that will last 15 to 20 minutes. There will be two parts.

Part A: You will prepare a short (five-minute) presentation, give the presentation and then answer questions about it.

Part B: You will role-play a networking situation at a conference.

A Choose one of the topics below and prepare a short presentation. You should begin with a suitable introduction, divide the information into about three main parts and end with a conclusion. You have 15 minutes to prepare.

1 Make a presentation about your own first impressions of a company, product or service. Provide a short background to the company, product or service, then explain the factors that created your first impression. Explain which good points should be preserved and areas in which you think the first impression could be improved.

2 Make a presentation about a job: either the job you have or one you would like to have. Describe the job in terms of current employment trends. What flexibility does the job allow? Does it involve working with 'virtual' teams that are geographically spread out? Does it involve working with both regular employees and short-term contract staff or consultants?

3 Make a presentation about any online aspect of your company's business. If your company actively does business online, explain how the business works: how the product or service is marketed, how orders are taken and filled, etc. If your company doesn't do business online, explain what function any online presence serves and explain why the company isn't well-suited to online business or how the company could make use of the Internet.

B Imagine you are at a conference waiting for a talk about doing business across cultures to begin. You decide to strike up a conversation with the person sitting next to you. Think of a topic you can introduce to get the conversation going and try to maintain the flow for about five minutes.

Audio scripts

The recordings of the material below can be found on the *Test Master* CD-ROM, which is at the back of the *Market Leader Third Edition Advanced Teacher's Resource Book*. They are also on the *Market Leader* website at www.market-leader.net. Play each recording twice.

Entry test

🔊 1

We focus today on four companies we believe could be targets for Oasis Organic Juice International's planned expansion. How have they been performing recently?

Let's start with Zumotina. Last year, it reported strong growth, with sales of $6 million and net profits increasing by 15.8 per cent. In the three previous years, turnover increased by 51 per cent and profits by 28 per cent. Zumotina has been very successful. Earlier this year, it introduced new 'pure juice' products which have been very popular.

Next, Good Juice, the UK company, is using all organic fruit to make high-end blended juices. Its main market is the UK but it also operates in the Netherlands. Last year, turnover was $8 million, with net profits of only $0.2 million. In the three previous years, profits grew by 7 per cent. Good Juice is planning to open a new plant in the near future.

Kimura Organic Fruit Products is another company Oasis Organic will probably be looking at. This Japanese company manufactures not only organic juices but also frozen fruit desserts. It also has several juice bars in Tokyo and Osaka. It could give Oasis Organic the opportunity to expand into Asia and to develop the juice bar segment of the market. Kimura, with sales last year of almost $9 million and net profits of $1 million, is a tempting target for Oasis Organic. The company grew fast in the previous three years, with profits increasing by 48 per cent.

Finally, will Oasis Organic go for a company near home? Some say they're taking a close look at Hightree Organic, based in Los Angeles, California. Hightree is one of the top manufacturers of organic juice products in North America; 95 per cent of its sales are in the home market but Hightree Organic also distributes in the UK. Sales topped $10 million last year, with net profits of $1 million. Profits have increased by less than 10 per cent in the last three years but the company has a strong position in the organic juice industry.

Progress test 1

🔊 **2** (I = Interviewer, HP = Helen Parker)

I How does a company know what kind of training it needs?

HP That's a good question. In fact, a lot of managers think that their teams need training in teamwork and a lot of employees think their managers need training. The hardest thing for any organisation to see is what they don't know. If you don't know something – if you don't know what's missing – how can you ask for it?

I I think I see what you mean. So how do you go about figuring out what sort of training to give?

HP I always go through a needs analysis process. This usually means I visit and observe a company for a few days. Sometimes I get them to do some activities that help me evaluate their values and understand their team dynamic.

I What sorts of things do you do?

HP Sometimes I give groups of people case studies to work on. A case study usually presents a problem or a dilemma in an organisation. There's no one correct answer or solution to these problems but it's always very interesting to see people's reactions. Sometimes, for example, people get really emotional and I can see what people are sensitive about.

I What else do you do?

HP Bridge-building and tower-building exercises are a good way to see how teams work together.

I Could you explain those?

HP Well, I give teams some basic supplies like cardboard and glue and I ask them to build something – a tower or a bridge – to certain specifications in a limited period of time. It's a good way to observe how leadership works, how people communicate and so on. I've found that team dynamics are pretty much the same whether people are playing a game or doing their job.

I Once you've seen a company in action, what happens next?

HP Most of the time I set up coaching programmes and sometimes I organise mentoring.

I What's the difference between coaching and mentoring?

HP Both are ways of working closely with people to improve skills that they already have. I usually arrange coaching for a fairly short period of time. Mentoring is a much longer-term process and it tends to require a relatively long-term investment by the person – someone already within the company – who's doing the mentoring and obviously it takes a lot of commitment from the person who's being mentored.

Progress test 2

🔊 3 (BW = Bill Wilson, AB = Alison Bates)

BW Can you spare a minute?

AB Sure. What's on your mind?

BW Work!

AB No surprise there! You busy?

BW Yeah, I am but that's not really the problem.

AB OK, well ... what's on your mind?

BW Well, it's ... it's Steve.

AB Steve?

BW Yeah, and listen, this conversation is just between you and me, right? I just want some advice.

AB Yeah, sure. Just between you and me.

BW Well, it's about expenses. Steve and I have been travelling together a lot and when we were in Seoul last month we were out checking out the displays in some of the international stores in a big shopping mall and Steve bought an expensive designer handbag while we were there.

AB Right ...

BW Well, it's just that he paid for it with his company credit card, which I noticed. Really it's none of my business but he told me the bag was for his wife and he also told me he had a good budget for client gifts and entertainment ...

AB And so he's buying presents for his wife with his company credit card.

BW Right. And not only that, he basically told me I should do the same thing and he told me how to submit my expenses so no one would notice.

AB Oh, dear. That's a tricky one!

BW I know. I mean, in a way, it's none of my business but, on the other hand, the whole company is trying to save money and it could really hurt the whole company if everyone used their company credit card this way. So I have to say, I feel tempted to go to Steve's manager and tell him what's going on.

AB Are you sure you really want to do that?

BW No, I'm not! I think Steve is doing a pretty good job and, if he left the company, it could really make a mess of things. Clients like him. He has a really good way with people.

AB Exactly. So you really do have to weigh up the pros and cons of talking with his boss. You might like to be ready for the next time it happens because you're bound to be in the same situation again.

BW That's true.

AB And when he uses his company credit card for something personal, you could tell him you've been thinking about it and you definitely don't want to use your company card in that way. The important thing is to avoid lecturing him about it or telling him what he's doing is wrong. If it were up to me, I'd raise the topic in a light way and at least get him thinking about what he's doing. You know Steve. Maybe he just hasn't thought through what he's doing.

BW Yeah, I think you're right. I mean, I don't think he'd steal anything from anyone if he thought of it as stealing. I'm sure he just thinks it's a kind of perk.

Progress test 3

🔊 4 (P = Pascal, K = Kate)

P Kate, how's it going?

K It's tough! How about you? Are you having any luck?

P It's been really tough. I've had conversations with people at 12 venture capital firms. They love the sound of our plan but every time we get to the question of experience and they find out we have none, that's basically the end of the conversation. I talked to one guy who said he wanted to set up a meeting but at the last minute he texted me to say he had to leave for Japan suddenly and had to cancel the meeting. And I haven't been able to get back in touch with him.

K That's tough.

P Yeah, I'm pretty down about it. What about you, Kate?

K I've basically had the same problems. I did manage to talk to one very helpful woman on the phone. She pointed out that most business angels don't want to splash out on a new business until it's actually making some money. She gave me two pieces of advice. One was to try to get as much funding as possible from friends and family to cover us until the business starts to take off. The other – and I think this is going to be really important – is to focus on finding customers. She says if we can find some good customers who really believe in us, it will help to convince investors that we have a good basis for the business.

P That sounds like good advice. But do we know anyone with enough money to get us started?

K Well, don't you remember that one of the first things I did was to ask my parents for help and they offered something like a thousand euros? Anyway, I wouldn't want to make them give away that kind of money so close to retirement. I mean, if it went wrong, they just can't afford to lose that much.

P Maybe we have to look beyond our parents. We could ask other relatives or friends of the family. If we each found ten people who could lend us a small amount, that would be a start, wouldn't it?

K Yeah, maybe. One thing I was wondering was whether we really need to raise a half million euros. If we look for less funding, we might be able to find it more easily.

P But how can we cut it back? We spent a huge amount of time on the business plan and worked out all the costs in detail – we didn't just dream up the half-million euro figure!

K Let's take another look. There must be ways to make some cuts. How about office rent? Do we really need to rent an office? Maybe we could work from home to begin with. Lots of successful entrepreneurs started out by working from a home office.

P That's right. And another thing: if we get investors to provide most of the backing – even supposing we can find people to do it – they're going to take control of our business. We'll have no say in how we run things. I'm not sure I want that.

K I agree. We should keep at least a 50 per cent stake for ourselves. Otherwise, we'll never make any money out of it.

Progress test 4

 5

The Critical Path Method is a technique for modelling projects and it's a fantastic tool for managing any kind of project. It's a type of mathematical analysis and it's commonly used in software development, research, engineering, plant maintenance, aerospace, … just about anything you can think of.

How does CPM work? To develop a model, you need three things. First, you need a detailed list of all of the activities that have to be done for the project to be completed. If you're building a house, this would include designing the house, putting in the foundations, doing the brick work, adding plumbing and electrics, and so on. Second, you need to know how much time each activity will take. The design phase might take six months, it might take a week to put in the foundations, and it may take a week for the electricians to do the first fix of the wiring. Finally, you need to know which activities depend on other activities. For the house-building project, you need to put the foundations in first, then build the frame on top of that, then add plumbing and electrics and so on.

Now we're ready to apply CPM. Given the values I just spoke about, CPM calculates the longest path of project activities from start to finish. It also determines the earliest that each activity can begin and the latest it can finish. This shows which activities are 'critical'. A critical activity is one that will affect the whole project if it's delayed. It also shows which activities have 'total float'. If an activity with 'total float' is delayed, it won't affect the completion date of the project.

So what's the 'critical path'? It's the sequence of activities required to complete the project and it shows the shortest possible time needed to complete the project. Any delay in an activity on the critical path will directly affect the end date of the project.

The usefulness of this model is obvious. It gives project managers the ability to prioritise activities, shorten their duration – we call this 'fast-tracking' – and apply resources to them for the maximum benefit of the project.

So what does a critical path actually look like? How can this information be displayed so it isn't too dense or complex? One way is a Gantt chart. A Gantt chart is a type of bar chart. It can have dates running along the top of the chart and a breakdown of project elements in a list at the left-hand side. For tracking work in progress, many Gantt charts include a vertical 'today' line so everyone can see exactly where the project stands.

Exit test

 6

I'd like to welcome you today to the newly-refurbished Daisy Hill Factory which you're going to get up and running over the next ten days.

At Talbot, it's not so much what we do as how we do it. There's a culture of excellence in this company. The firm is no longer owned by the Talbot family but for half of the nineteenth and most of the twentieth century it was. The Talbots didn't believe in standing still and, in a highly competitive market, there's no room for complacency. We've always actively looked for ways of improving, have always asked 'Is our organisation running as smoothly as it should? Could we do more to improve the dialogue we have with our customers? Could we improve services?' Those are the questions we have to keep answering to keep moving forward and those are questions that we think everyone in the company should be thinking about every day. Often the best ideas for how to improve efficiency have come from the men and women on the factory floor because you're the ones who really know what's going on.

So where is Talbot going? What's the goal we're all trying to reach? We have three main targets that we're always trying to hit. One is to develop and maintain long-standing relationships with our customers. We have to work closely with them or we can't develop products for them. The best work often comes from two companies sharing ideas and expertise rather than a client just coming to us with an order to make something. In fact, that's one way we differentiate ourselves in the market: the way we involve customers in our R and D. This means you can expect frequent visits from clients so they can see what we're doing and how we're doing it.

Another target we never lose sight of is the need to manage production costs, keeping in mind that people are a huge part of that. As our equipment gets older and becomes less efficient we at times need to move production from one factory to another. The key to managing the human side of this is not to show up one day and say 'Sorry, we're closing your assembly line next week, you have to leave.' We're often looking ahead ten years to equipment replacement and this sort of planning helps us manage the human resources angle of closures.

The third target we have is to become more multinational. Currently, 40 per cent of our sales go outside the UK. But there are huge markets out there. Look at China. There are more than a billion people there, some of whom could be using our products in ten years' time – if we play our cards right. Part of the plan is to build plants in India and China. We already have joint ventures with local partners and more are in the planning stages. Does this mean eventually outsourcing your jobs to Asia? No, it doesn't. We have expertise here in the UK that we are committed to maintaining. Some of you will have the opportunity to work for periods of time in our new facilities abroad as part of training up workers there in our culture of excellence.

Guidelines for the examiner

Examiner's notes: Writing tests

For each writing task award a maximum of 15 marks, as follows.

For the Entry test
- Use of appropriate letter style and politeness: 5 marks
- Overall clarity and coherence: 5 marks
- Grammatical accuracy (deduct half a mark for each serious mistake): 5 marks

For the Progress and Exit tests
- Overall clarity and coherence: 6 marks
- Grammatical accuracy (deduct half a mark for each serious mistake): 3 marks
- Use of appropriate style: 3 marks
- Use of appropriate linkers: 3 marks

Examiner's notes: Speaking

It is recommended that the speaking tests be recorded on tape for analysis afterwards. Oral performance should always be assessed by at least two teachers. In the event of disagreement, award a score midway between the two (if two assessors) or take an average (if three or more assessors).

The oral performance of candidates with a score of 8 or more can be described as follows:

The candidate can use English to communicate effectively and consistently, with few hesitations or uncertainties.

Description based on level 7 of the English Speaking Union's Framework of Examination Levels.

Entry test

This test should take 10 to 15 minutes per candidate. Candidates each give a short (five-minute) presentation and then answer your questions about it.

Allow candidates five minutes to prepare. While one candidate is being tested, the next one can prepare their presentation.

Notes on assessment

Award a maximum of 15 marks, 3 marks each for of the following criteria.
- Fluency and confidence
- Overall comprehensibility (including clear pronunciation)
- Accuracy and appropriateness of language
- Ability to organise ideas and structure the presentation
- Range of language (grammar, functional phrases, vocabulary)

Exit test

This test should take 15 to 20 minutes per candidate. There are two parts.
- Part A: A short (five-minute) presentation
- Part B: A role-play of a conversation with someone you meet at a conference.

Allow candidates 15 minutes to prepare. While one candidate is being tested, the next one can prepare for their presentation.

Notes for carrying out each part

Presentation

After listening to the candidate's presentation, ask two or three questions about the content or anything missing from the content. You should ask one fairly difficult question to see how the candidate deals with it.

Role-play

This can be done in two ways: either you play the second role or two candidates can be tested at the same time by asking them to role-play in pairs. If you take part in the role-play yourself, be careful not to help the candidate too much. As far as possible, the candidate should take control of the conversation: making a start, introducing topics and keeping it moving. You contribute appropriate responses, questions or comments.

Notes on assessment

Presentation

Award a maximum of 5 marks, 1 mark each for the following criteria.
- Fluency, confidence and a strong, enthusiastic delivery
- Overall comprehensibility (including clear pronunciation)
- Accuracy and appropriateness of language
- Ability to organise ideas and structure the presentation
- Range of language (grammar, functional phrases, vocabulary)

Role-play

Award a maximum of 10 marks, as follows.
- Ability to respond quickly and appropriately to the other person: 4 marks
- Ability to engage readily in conversation about a variety of topics: 3 marks
- Ability to keep the conversation moving without hesitations or unnatural pauses: 3 marks

Pearson Education Limited
Edinburgh Gate
Harlow
Essex CM20 2JE
England
and Associated Companies throughout the world.

www.market-leader.net

First published 2006
Third edition 2011
Thirteenth impression 2019

ISBN 978-1-4082-1963-8

Set in Metaplus 9.5/12.5pt
Printed by Ashford Colour Press Ltd.

Project managed by Chris Hartley

Acknowledgements

We are grateful to the following for permission to reproduce copyright material:

Text

Extract in Exit test Reading from "The careerist: 'The key to ambition is
understanding your motivations'", The Financial Times, 24/05/2010
(Rhymer Rigby), copyright © Rhymer Rigby.

The Financial Times

Extract in Entry test Language A adapted from "Opel aims for growth outside
Europe", The Financial Times, 30/09/2010 (Schäfer, D.), copyright © The Financial
Times Ltd; Extract in Entry test Reading from "Some home truths about doing
business abroad", The Financial Times, 06/09/2010 (Moules, J.), copyright © The
Financial Times Ltd; Extract in Progress test 1 Reading adapted from "Renewable
energy: Cloudy forecast for solar power", The Financial Times, 05/10/2010
(Mulligan, M.), copyright © The Financial Times Ltd; Extract in Progress test 2
Reading from "Staff motivation misunderstood", The Financial Times, 20/09/2010
(Groom, B.), copyright © The Financial Times Ltd; Extract in Progress test 3
Reading adapted from "Government spends £1.5bn on consultants", The Financial
Times, 13/10/2010 (Timmins, N.), copyright © The Financial Times Ltd; and
Extract in Progress test 4 Reading from "Find the finance – and hold your nerve",
The Financial Times, 31/10/2010 (Moules, J.), copyright © The Financial Times Ltd.